Natural Cleaning Recipes

Non Toxic Products for the Eco Friendly Home

By: Karen S. Roberts

Public Library District of Columbia

TABLE OF CONTENTS

Karen S. Roberts

PUBLISHERS NOTES

Disclaimer

This publication is intended to provide helpful and informative material. It is not intended to diagnose, treat, cure, or prevent any health problem or condition, nor is intended to replace the advice of a physician. No action should be taken solely on the contents of this book. Always consult your physician or qualified health-care professional on any matters regarding your health and before adopting any suggestions in this book or drawing inferences from it.

The author and publisher specifically disclaim all responsibility for any liability, loss or risk, personal or otherwise, which is incurred as a consequence, directly or indirectly, from the use or application of any contents of this book.

Any and all product names referenced within this book are the trademarks of their respective owners. None of these owners have sponsored, authorized, endorsed, or approved this book.

Always read all information provided by the manufacturers' product labels before using their products. The author and publisher are not responsible for claims made by manufacturers.

© 2013

Manufactured in the United States of America

DEDICATION

This book is dedicated to those who wish to do their part to save the planet.

CHAPTER 1- WHAT DOES IT MEAN TO DO NATURAL CLEANING?

Natural cleaning has made quite a breakthrough in the past few years. The process of natural cleaning entails using all natural, environmentally friendly, safe, toxic free products. Consumers no longer want to purchase harmful household chemicals to clean their home. Not only are these chemicals unsafe for pets and children, but they can even be more costly than some natural cleaners that can do the job just as good, if not better.

There are so many cleaning products on the market today that can emit volatile compounds which can cause respiratory and dermatological complications. Natural cleaning can also describe the way a cleaning product is packaged and distributed. If a cleaning product is biodegradable and environmentally safe then it can be labeled as "clean", "green", or "eco-friendly". This chapter will cover some natural cleaning solutions that you can use to clean your home safely and effectively. No more need for toxic chemicals to clean your house!

Vinegar

Vinegar can safely clean so many things in your home. You can clean your windows by mixing 1/4 cup of vinegar and two cups of water in a spray bottle. Spray windows with this solution and wipe them off with newspaper and you will safely clean all the windows in your home. Have a smelly dishwasher? Pour some vinegar in the reservoir and then run and empty cycle. Vinegar can also clean your floors (except wood) by adding 1/4 cup of vinegar to a big container or bucket of warm water. No more need to buy a toxic drain cleaning solution either! Vinegar can also clean and unclog any drains you may have. Just add a small amount of baking soda and pour some vinegar down the pipes on top of the baking soda. You will see it fizz and bubble and know it is doing its job.

Baking Soda

Baking soda is a great alternative to many harmful cleaners on the market today. Baking soda can be used to clean floors by mixing a 1/2 cup into a bucket of warm water. Mop away and see your floor shine! You can get a cleaner load of laundry by adding one cup along with your regular laundry detergent and watch how clean your clothes will get. Use baking soda to make your own bathroom cleaner by mixing 1/4 a cup of baking soda with one tablespoon of liquid detergent. Add a few drops of vinegar until it becomes a thick texture, then scrub away. This can clean your entire bathroom sink, tub, and toilet without any harsh chemicals or toxic smells. Do you hate the smell of your cat's litter box? Add some baking soda to the box, and then place the litter over the baking soda. The baking soda will keep the litter box smelling fresher longer than usual.

Lemons

Karen S. Roberts

You would be amazed at what lemons can do! Lemons can remove dirt and rust due to the acid in their juice. Lemons can kill the lime scale on faucets just by rubbing some lemon juice onto the faucet. Let the juice sit on the faucet over night, the next morning just wipe it off and see how it shines! Lemons can also cut grease stains from dishes and Tupperware just by mixing a teaspoon of lemon juice to your dish detergent.

Castile Soap

Castile soap is an all natural plant based soap that is gentle and effectively loosens dirt from surfaces. You can use liquid Castile soap to clean almost anything including floors, cars, countertops, to stovetops and showers. Just mix a tablespoon of soap with a bucket of warm water to clean just about any surface and this soap will kill unwanted grease or grime. For a clean car, you can mix 1/4 cup of soap with a bucket of hot water and it will clean your tires, hood, hubcaps, windshield and entire car without hurting your car's exterior paint.

Cooking Oils

Cooking oils are great at naturally cleaning wood surfaces. To clean wood furniture, mix two cups of olive oil with the juice of one lemon. This mixture will smooth out any scratches that the furniture may have and make it look like new. Cooking oils can also clean any cast-iron pans you may have. Just mix some vegetable oil with a little bit of salt, scrub the pan, and rinse away with water.

Toothpaste

Toothpaste can work as a mild abrasive. It can be very similar to a soft scrub solution. It can be used to clean jewelry by dabbing a small amount on an old toothbrush and brush away. You will see how the toothpaste can instantly shine the jewelry. Allowing the toothpaste to soak overnight on old pieces of jewelry with tough stains is an even better idea. In the morning, just rinse it off and polish it dry to see how beautiful it looks. Toothpaste can also remove crayon marks on the walls. Just rub a bit of toothpaste on a damp cloth and wipe away. You will see it easily remove the crayon marks without damaging your walls. It can also clean those old and grimy looking piano keys. Scrub those piano keys with a little bit of toothpaste and watch how white they become.

Using any of the above household items to clean your home means that you are cleaning naturally. Natural cleaning may surprise you once you see how effective it can be to use basic baking soda and vinegar to clean some of the dirtiest things in your home. It will not only be safe for your family and pets but will also save you money. Average household cleaning products on the market today can get costly and can be used up so quickly. Things like lemons, baking soda, vinegar, and toothpaste are most items you already have in your home and can be purchased at a much lower price than some chemical cleaning products. Give some of these natural cleaning products a try for a safer home and environment.

Karen S. Roberts

CHAPTER 2- WHAT ARE THE BENEFITS OF USING NATURAL CLEANING RECIPES?

As more persons pay attention to the numerous health and environmental issues facing them today, there is a growing interest in natural cleaning methods. Most commercially available cleaning products are made with chemicals that are now known to be dangerous to people, animals and the planet. If you've found yourself wondering how you can keep your home clean and smelling nice without employing hazardous substances, it's easier than you might think.

Many common household products can be used, and you likely already have some of them in your pantry or refrigerator. White vinegar works as an effective alternative to bleach for sanitizing surfaces. Baking soda can be used in place of harsh scouring cleansers. Things like lemon juice, citrus oils and many herbs are a great way to freshen the air, and some even discourage bacterial growth. What's more, these things can be mixed safely to create stronger cleaners. Here are some of the major benefits of using natural cleaning recipes.

Environmental Safety and Preservation

When people use conventional cleaners, these products eventually wind up in the environment through a variety of means. When they're rinsed or poured down drains, they contaminate waterways, killing aquatic life or causing severe mutations. The cleaners can also contaminate municipal water sources, forcing you to drink and bathe in chemical residues. When partly full packages of cleaners are thrown away, they end up in landfills, where they inevitably leach into the soil. This poses a threat to plants and wild animals as well as groundwater supplies. Meanwhile, natural cleaners don't pose any environmental threat. They're quickly and harmlessly neutralized or broken down into their base elements.

Human Health

One of the biggest concerns homeowners have with standard cleaning products are the health risks to themselves and their families. An average home can harbor around 25 gallons of poisonous chemicals, most of them in the form of cleaning products. To make matters worse, US law doesn't force companies to list these ingredients since they're considered trade secrets. Indeed, the government has laws in place that actively protect companies from having to reveal this information to consumers. That said there are some substances you can count on being in those cleaners:

Corrosives and irritants like ammonia, chlorine and hydrochloric acid

Endocrine disruptors like petroleum, synthetic fragrances, BPA, alkylphenols and parabens

Lead, mercury, aluminum and other heavy metals known to cause birth defects, developmental disorders, behavioral problems, neurological issues and organ damage

Of course, this isn't a concern with natural products. In many cases, natural cleaners can actually benefit your health rather than compromise it. Vinegar is great for your skin, baking soda counteracts many skin irritants and certain herbal fragrances have been shown to promote a good mood.

Pet Health

People with pets also have to think about their furry friends when using cleaners. Most ready-made products are severely toxic to cats and dogs, information that isn't always indicated on the packaging. In fact, there have been numerous cases throughout the years of supposedly safe products, mainly floor cleaners, killing pets by the dozens, resulting in several major lawsuits. In contrast, things like lemon juice, tea tree oil or vinegar pose absolutely no risk to animals, making them safe alternative for concerned pet parents.

Petroleum Independence

Because most conventional cleaning products are made from petrochemicals, they only encourage the country's dependence on oil. Furthermore, manufacturing these petrochemicals means a lot of refining, which inevitably creates harmful air pollution and by-products that have to be stored or disposed of. By using the natural options available in your own pantry, you can help reduce the nation's reliance on petroleum.

Air Quality

When it comes to toxic products, you have more to worry about than just the unpleasant smell. You also have to worry about what they're doing to your indoor air quality. Many of these substances stay in the air long after you're finished using them, where they're being constantly inhaled by everyone in your household. Some things, like air fresheners, are even designed to be this way. This can result in worsened allergies and other respiratory problems. When you clean with what nature has already provided, you don't have to be concerned about poisoning the air you breathe.

Savings

A stroll down your store's household needs aisle will quickly add insult to injury. Not only are the products dangerous but also ludicrously expensive. Instead, stick to the aisles where foods are sold, because it's here that you'll save money. Simple products like vinegar or baking soda cost pennies, making it easier to control a tight budget.

Availability and Ease of Use

Natural cleaning options are just as easy to use as conventional ones. In most cases, they can be diluted with water and added to a spray bottle, or they can be made into a paste and used. They're also just as widely available, if not more so. Take a look through your cabinets. Most people already possess the means to clean their entire home right in their cupboards.

Peace of Mind

There are cleaning products being sold that claim to be natural or Earth-friendly. However, the companies expect you to take this labeling at face value, since they're also not required to list ingredients. Disturbingly, analyses of some popular "natural" cleaners have revealed that they do contain known toxins and

Karen S. Roberts

carcinogens. Some have even been found to be harmful to animals. Meanwhile, nobody can question the safety of things like vinegar or lemons, and you know exactly what's in them.

Making a Difference

Using truly natural cleaning recipes sends a strong message to corporations that people are no longer interested in their dangerous or questionable products. As more people move toward this line of thinking, companies will have to start paying attention. Eventually, better, safer and more natural products will become cheaper and more widely available.

All-Purpose

One of the greatest things about natural cleaners is that they can be used for any and all surfaces in your home, regardless of the material. Because they're mild, non-corrosive and don't stain, you can use them to polish chrome, remove hard water buildup, clean glass, dust furniture and scour stoves, sinks and tubs. Some even make highly effective carpet and garbage disposal deodorizers.

When it comes time for another housekeeping spree, don't be so quick to reach for that bottle of blue window cleaner or can mysterious bleach-scented powder. Instead, open your cabinets and see what you have available. The things you can do with what's there may surprise you.

CHAPTER 3- WHY SHOULD CHEMICAL BASED CLEANING PRODUCTS NOT BE USED?

When you clean your home, you want to make sure that it is impeccably clean. You try out new cleaning products as they become available on the market. This is mostly because there are new advances on germ control in the home. You buy cleaning products that you think will help keep your home spotless and pretty much germ free. You clean your home with these products to make sure that your family doesn't get sick. Do you know that you could be causing illnesses by using these chemical cleaners?

When you clean your home, do you use the chemical cleaners that your parents have used in the past, or do you use cleaners that are more natural and safer for your home and your environment? Chances are that you use the chemical cleaners that your parents have used in the past. As mentioned in previous chapters, unfortunately, these can be very harmful to your health and the health of those around you. They can also be very harmful for your environment.

Chemical cleaners have been proven to be very hazardous to your home and your health. Natural cleaners that contain ingredients that are easy to read can be more helpful to your health and home. While chemical cleaners are good for cleaning and disinfecting your home, they give off an odor and other gases that can be very hazardous to all of your family members. This even includes pets. Some cleaning products can be hazardous by touching them. They can cause irritation to your eyes, nose, throat, and lungs. They cause cold like symptoms or make you feel as though you have the flu.

Karen S. Roberts

Recent studies have shown that cleaning agents can cause severe allergies. They can also cause severe irritation to your respiratory system and your skin. Sometimes you can even get a chemical burn from using cleaners without any protective gear. If you use these chemical cleaners for a long period of time, you could be at a higher risk for developing cancer.

There have been certain chemicals like bleach and ammonia that can cause lung damage because of the high amount of fumes they give off. It can also be lethal to people who have asthma to be using these chemical products because it can damage their lungs more and set up an asthmatic reaction.

When using chemical cleaners, it is highly recommended that you wear protective gear. Some include a mask, rubber gloves, and an apron to keep the cleaners from spilling on your clothing. It is important to wear these protective elements to safeguard yourself from the harmful chemicals that you are exposing to yourself. If you choose not to follow these protective measurements, you are putting yourself in more danger and could ultimately cause yourself to be seriously sick.

Not only are there chemicals that can be hazardous to your health, but some fragrances that are added to your laundry detergent or fabric softener can be hazardous as well. These fragrances can cause irritation to the skin as well as irritation to your respiratory system. Most companies don't share what their fragrances are because they aren't required to. This makes it difficult to take these out of your home. The only way to remove it from your home is to not use any detergent or fabric softeners with a fragrance in them. If you do use a detergent or fabric softener that has a fragrance, make sure to use one that has a natural fragrance and shows the ingredients for the fragrance on the label. That is the only way that you can be sure that you will be getting something that is more natural.

Some household cleaners have what is called hormone disruptors that can confuse the body's messages throughout the body. They have been known to cause decreased sperm count, cancer in men, and undescended testicles in newborn males. Some also imitate estrogen that can cause breast cancer in women. They can cause asthmatic reactions as well as burns, and flu symptoms.

Not only are these chemical cleaners bad for our homes, they are bad for our environment as well. They mix with our sewage and other harmless substances. Some even ruin the quality of the water that our fish live in and our wildlife drink from. More than 50% of our water in the United States has been contaminated with the remains of laundry detergents or other cleaners. This means that more than half of our water sources contain remnants of someone's laundry soap, dish soap, or other chemical that has been used in a cleaner. This also affects our soil.

Some chemicals in cleaners are so toxic that they kill everything that is living in the water supply. This includes fish, algae, fish eggs, and other creatures that live in the water. It can be even more harmful to the animals that eat the fish and human beings that catch the fish.

So, what can you use that isn't harmful to your home or to your community? Using all natural cleaners can be tricky. Some say that they are all natural but still have chemicals that can be harmful to your family. Make sure that you read the ingredients on the bottle. If you can read all the ingredients and understand what they are, then it is an all-natural product. There are many household cleaning products that are safe to use and inexpensive at the same time.

With these environmentally safe cleaners, you also receive an environmentally safe container. Most cleaners that are safe to use contain vinegar, baking soda, lemon juice or other natural agents. Mixing these ingredients together can help clean any surface in your home safely and make it germ free at the same time. The best part is that you can find recipes online that can help you make your own cleaners using these three ingredients to help make your home germ free and spic and span. You just need to purchase a reusable container to keep your mixture in, lemon juice, baking soda, and vinegar.

CHAPTER 4- 10 NATURAL CLEANING RECIPES FOR THE HOME

People today have become increasingly concerned with using harsh chemicals to clean their homes. Many of the products on the market come with health warnings and can be dangerous if used near children or pets. More people are seeking out natural home cleaners to do the jobs that they previously used store bought products to clean. If you are interested in switching some or all of your cleaning products to natural products, there are some very basic ingredients that you should keep on hand to make your cleaning easier.

Natural Cleaning Ingredients

Baking Soda
Corn Starch
Kosher Salt
Borax
White Vinegar
Hydrogen Peroxide
Citrus Fruit - Lemons, Grapefruit
Essential Oils - Orange Oil
Olive Oil

Equipment that you may need

Spray bottle
Microfiber cloth
Sponges
Small container with lid
Scrub pads
Old toothbrush

Karen S. Roberts

Greasy Grime Cleaner

Ingredients

White Vinegar
Baking Soda
Orange Oil

Directions

Simply spray or pour white vinegar onto the greasy surface and leave it sit for 10 minutes, then simply wipe the grease and vinegar away. If the vinegar doesn't get it all, add some baking soda to a sponge and scrub the grease like you would use an abrasive cleaner to remove it. If that is still doesn't get it all, add a small amount of orange oil to the sponge and rub over it until it is all gone.

Kitchen Disinfectant

Ingredients

½ cup of Baking Soda
½ cup of White Vinegar
One pot of boiling water

Directions

Pour 1/2 cup of baking soda into the drain while it is dry, then pour 1/2 cup of white vinegar into the drain. There will be a chemical reaction; a lot of bubbles should boil up out of the drain. Allow this to sit for 5 to 10 minutes, and then pour boiling hot water down the drain to rinse the residue away. CAUTION! You should NOT use this method if you have already used a chemical drain cleaner in the drain as there would be dangerous fumes as a result.

Carpet Freshener

Ingredients

1 cup of Baking Soda
1 cup of Corn Starch

Directions

Mix the baking soda and the corn starch together well. Then just before you go to bed, sprinkle liberally onto your carpet and leave it over night. When you wake up the next day vacuum the carpet, it will smell fresh and clean. The added bonus is that once the baking soda gets into the vacuum, it will freshen it as well.

Glass Cleaner

Ingredients

1 Lemon
1 liter of Water

Directions

Juice the lemon and add it to one liter of water. Wash the windows with the mixture and use a crumpled up black and white newspaper to buff it dry. Make sure not to clean windows that are in direct sunlight as the heat causes the windows to streak.

Tip:

If you have problems with streaks, wash one side of the window from top to bottom then wash the other side from side to side. This way if there are streaks you will be able to tell which side they are on to wipe them away.

Wood Cleaner

Karen S. Roberts

Ingredients

1 Lemon
2 Tablespoons of Olive Oil

Directions

Juice the lemon and strain out the seeds and pulp. Pour the juice into a container with a lid. Add 2 Tablespoons of olive oil. Shake vigorously for a few minutes to mix well. Dampen a microfiber cloth with the mixture and clean your wooden furniture with it. Throw away any leftover mixture because it will go bad after a few days.

Grout Cleaner

Ingredients

1-2 Lemons
½ cup of Baking Soda

Directions

Cut the lemons into quarters. Dip the edge of the lemon into some baking soda and rub vigorously onto the grout to moisten. Leave it sit for a few minutes, then rinse. If the grout is very dirty it may require scrubbing with an old toothbrush or a grout brush. This will brighten up old dingy grout.

Bathtub and Shower Cleaner

Ingredients

1 Grapefruit
¼ cup of Kosher Salt

Directions

Cut the grapefruit in half. Wet the bathtub. Sprinkle half of the kosher salt into the bathtub. Use half of the grapefruit with salt on it to scrub the bathtub. Make sure to clean the fixtures as well. Do the same with the other half of the grapefruit then rinse off all of the salt and grapefruit pulp. For showers, use the same technique.

Sanitize Your Bathroom

Ingredients

1 cup of Hydrogen Peroxide
1 cup of Water

Directions

Mix 1 cup of hydrogen peroxide with 1 cup of water, pour it into a spray bottle and use it throughout your bathroom (especially around the toilet) to sanitize it. Simply spray on and wipe off with a clean cloth. You don't want to make too much in advance as the peroxide will go bad in sunlight.

Tip:

Wait for a bottle of hydrogen peroxide to be half empty, add the other half of water and attach a spray top to the peroxide bottle. You can continue to use this bottle for your solution as long as you like.

Toilet Bowl Cleaner

Ingredients

2 Tablespoons of Borax
½ a Lemon

Karen S. Roberts
Directions

Mix the juice from the half a lemon with the borax. Pour the mixture into the toilet bowl and scrub as usual. Let sit for a few minutes to help remove stubborn stains; to help keep the toilet clean try running the brush over it every couple days with a sprinkle of borax. It will prevent stains from forming.

By using these natural cleaning recipes, you will be able to keep the chemicals at bay. Once you become used to using them, you will instinctively know which ingredient will clean the fastest and the safest. The best part is as well as being clean; your house will smell fresh all day.

CHAPTER 5- 10 NATURAL CLEANING RECIPES FOR LAUNDRY

Getting clothes dirty and having to do the laundry is a cycle that seems to never end. In order to clean your clothes, you need to use some sort of laundry soap or detergent and if desired, some sort of laundry softener.

In today's world, many people are trying to help preserve the economy by using more natural products instead of the harsh chemicals that are found in some types of commercial laundry products. If you would rather save money and help keep the environment safer, cleaner, then try out some of these natural cleaning recipes for laundry:

Liquid Laundry Detergent Recipe

Ingredients/Materials

⅓ a bar of soap
½ cup of washing soda
½ cup of borax power
6 cups of water
1 gallon of water and six more cups of water

Stock Pot
Five gallon bucket

Directions

Take a grater and shave the bar of soap into small pieces and put the pieces in the stock pot. Then, pour in the first six cups of water and place the stock pot on the stove at low heat until the soap gets melted. Next, add in the washing soda and borax. Stir the mixture

Karen S. Roberts

until it is dissolves. Take off heat and pour it into the bucket. Add the other water slowly and stir until it mixes totally. Then, it must sit for 24 hours until it gels. To use, take one half cup of the mixture for each load of laundry.

Dry Laundry Powder Recipe

Ingredients

1 bar of shaved soap
1 cup of borax
1 cup of washing soda

Directions

Mix up all of the ingredients and put it into an appropriate container. You only need to use one tablespoon of the mixture for each load of laundry.

Love It! Laundry Powder

Ingredients

1 cup of distilled white vinegar
1 cup of baking soda
1 cup of washing soda
¼ quarter cup of castile soap

Directions

Put the castile soap into a big bowl. Then, put in the washing soda, stir, and add the baking soda and stir again. Next, add the distilled vinegar slowly, as it will cause the mixture to foam. Then, it will start to form a paste, but keep on stirring until it starts to form a powder. Be sure to break up any lumps.

Next, it must sit for 30 minutes. In that time it will start to look more like a regular powdered laundry detergent. It must be kept in a sealed container. To use, take one half cup of powder for each laundry load. To keep your first load from turning yellow, run the first load with a third cup of washing soda to get rid of any residue from your old detergent.

Another Natural Laundry Detergent

Ingredients/Material

¼ bar of grated up soap
1 cup of boiling water
3 quarts or additional water
2 tablespoons of borax
¼ cup of washing soda

Bucket

Directions

Totally dissolve the cup of soap pieces into the boiling water. Completely dissolve the grated soap in the boiling water. Then, put the other water into a bucket and add in the mixture and stir it up. It will be rather goopy and you will use a third of a cup of it for each load of laundry.

Homemade Fabric Softener

Ingredients/Materials:

1 cup of baking soda
6 cups of distilled white vinegar
8 cups of water
Essential oil (optional)

Karen S. Roberts

Large bucket with a spout
Bottles to store it in

Directions

Add baking soda to the bucket and then add a cup of water and stir it all up. Add the vinegar slowly, as it will cause the mixture to foam. Then, add in the rest of the water. Pour the mixture into storage bottles and add several drops of whatever scent of essential oils you desire or leave it unscented. You will use one cup of the mixture during the rinse cycle of a load of laundry.

Several More Homemade Fabric Softener Recipes

Here are several additional homemade fabric softener laundry recipes for you to try instead of using commercial fabric softeners.

Vinegar Liquid Fabric Softener

Ingredients

¼ cup of white vinegar
20 drops of essential oil of your choice

Directions

Mix up the essential oil into the vinegar and use the whole thing during the final rinse of the laundry cycle.

Alternate Vinegar Fabric Softener

Ingredients

1 cup of vinegar
2 tablespoons of baking soda
Essential Oil of your choice

Directions

Mix it all together and put into a container. Shake prior to using and put one quarter cup of the mixture in the laundry during the rinse cycle.

Baking Soda Fabric Softener

Ingredient

½ cup of baking soda

Directions: Just put a half cup of baking soda into the washing machine water prior to adding the clothes to be washed.

Homemade Fabric Softener Sheets

Ingredients/Materials

1 cup of white vinegar
Essential Oil of your choice
Small pieces of cotton cloth

Directions

Soak the clothes in the mixture of vinegar and essential oil. Wring them out and put one cloth into the dryer for each load of laundry.

Citrus Laundry Fabric Softener Sheets

Ingredients/Materials

Lemon or lime juice (this can be either fresh or bottled juice)
2 Tablespoons of baking soda
Small Pieces of Cotton Cloths

Directions

Stir the baking soda into the juice and wait until it dissolves. Then, soak the cotton cloths into the mixture. Wring them out and put one cloth into the dryer for each load of laundry.

All and all there are many different natural and homemade recipes you can try for doing laundry that work well to clean your clothing and make it smell fresh and sweet. Be sure to try each of the above laundry recipes and see which one works best for you. You will be saving money as well as helping to preserve the environment by using natural laundry cleaning supplies.

CHAPTER 6- 10 NATURAL CLEANING RECIPES FOR STAIN REMOVAL

Stains are a part of everyday life whether someone drops a glass of red wine onto a white carpet, the cat hacks up a hairball on your pants or the baby throws up on his outfit. Whatever the stain, there are several ways to clean it with, including both chemical and natural stain removal products. While most people seem to automatically grab some sort of chemical based commercial stain remover, there are good reasons to choose natural cleaning options instead.

Natural stain removal options are better for the environment and are also gentler on your clothes or rug as well. They are less irritating and also fewer chemicals will get released into the environment. Plus, if someone has an allergy, the natural products are also better for their usage as they are less likely to cause problems.

You can easily make your own natural cleaning products for stain removal and here are 10 easy recipes to start you off:

Here are 10 natural cleaning recipes for stain removal:

Simple Lemon Stain Removal

Ingredients/Materials

1½ cups water
¼ cup liquid castile soap
¼ cup liquid vegetable glycerin
Lemon Essential Oil (five to 10 drops)
Glass Spray Bottle

Instructions

Mix up all of the ingredients and put the combination into a glass spray bottle and shake it up (lemon oil causes plastic to disintegrate so it can't be used it in a plastic one). When using it just apply it onto the stain and let it soak in overnight for best results. Then, clean the clothing or rug normally.

Homemade Bleach

Ingredients/Materials

1 cup of hydrogen peroxide
3 tablespoons of lemon juice
15 cups of water

Large jug or several smaller spray bottles

Directions

Mix up all of the ingredients and put it into a large container. You can also split it up into small spray bottles later for easier usage. This mixture needs to be used within 30 days because the peroxide loses strength due to oxidation. Just spray it liberally onto the stained area and blot it up to clean it or if it is clothing, then launder it normally.

Homemade OxyClean

Ingredients

1 cup of water
½ of hydrogen peroxide
½ cup of baking soda

Directions

Mix up all of the ingredients and put it into a container. It can be uses it by soaking the stained laundry in it at least 20 minutes or as long as overnight for best results. Then, wash the clothes normally.

Citrus Stain Cleaning Liquid

Ingredients/Materials

2 Liter Wide Mouth Bottle
2 cups peels from lemons, limes, or oranges
½ cup brown or white sugar
1 teaspoon active yeast
Strainer
1 cup apple cider vinegar (for after enzyme has fermented
1 liter of water

Instructions

Chop up the citrus peels and put them into the bottle. You need enough to fill it up about halfway. Add in the sugar, water, and yeast and shake it up for half a minute. Put a lid on the bottle loosely. In about two days there will be foam in the bottle due to the yeast fermenting. Shake the bottle once every day to mix up the yeast and let some air out of the bottle.

In about two weeks it turns opaque in color. Then it's time to strain the peels and pulp out of the mixture. After that, you can add the vinegar and then put the mixture into a glass jar to store it. To make a spray stain remover, mix it at a 1 to 10 ratio with the mix and water and put it into a spray bottle.

To use it, spray it on the stains and let sit for 20 to 30 minutes and then wash as you would normally.

Laundry Stain Remover

Ingredients/Materials

Toothbrush
White Vinegar
Washing soda or Borax
Water

Directions

Add Washing Soda or Borax to a container that has holes in the top so it can be shaken easier. Mix the white vinegar one to one with water in a spray bottle. When you are ready to use it on a stain, shake out some washing powder or borax onto the stain, then spray the stain with the vinegar mixture. Scrub it in with the toothbrush. Wait about 20 minutes and wash regularly.

Homemade Shout Pre-Treatment

Ingredients

⅔ cup Dawn dish detergent
⅔ cup ammonia

33

6 tablespoons baking soda

2 cups warm water

Directions

Mix it all up, and then put it into a spray bottle. Shake well before using and spray on stains as needed. Don't mix it with bleach because bleach and ammonia mixed together are dangerous! Let the stain sit for several minutes and then launder normally.

Mix for Heavy Duty Stains

Ingredients

¼ cup of salt

¼ cup of borax

¼ cup of vinegar

Directions

Mix together, rub some into the stained areas and clean normally. You can let it sit for several minutes or overnight if desired.

Spot Remover

Ingredients

1 tablespoon of white vinegar

1 tablespoon of baking soda

1 tablespoon of water

Directions

Mix as needed the amount for the size of the stain and make a paste to rub into the stain. Let dry and then vacuum it. Repeat as needed to get rid of stains.

Karen S. Roberts
Light Spot Removal Liquid

Ingredients

¼ cup of white vinegar (can also use ammonia instead of white vinegar)
1 cup of warm water

Directions

Mix it all up and put it into a spray bottle and spray on stains and blot it with paper towels to remove the stains. Or spray on clothing stains and let sit for a few minutes before doing the laundry.

Mixture for Deep Stains

Ingredients

¼ cup of salt
¼ cup of borax
¼ cup of white vinegar

Directions

Mix it up and make a paste to rub into stained areas. Leave on for several hours and vacuum off. This is good for carpeting.

CHAPTER 7- WHY CARE HAS TO BE TAKEN WHEN SELECTING CLEANING PRODUCTS

As mentioned in the previous chapters some basic ingredients like borax, lemon juice, vinegar, baking soda, water and soap along with a few other tools like a sponge and some manpower, is able to deal with most of the cleaning requirements for the home and office. In addition to that they are not expensive and will end up saving you a lot of money. For that reason alone the recipes were provided to give you a head start.

There are some instances however, that will require the use of some of the commercially made cleaners. It may be as simple as some dishwashing detergent or laundry detergent. Outlined below are some things that you should bear in mind if you are to keep cleaning green and not damage the environment any further or put your health at risk.

Even though a lot of the cleaners out there do not have their ingredients listed, you can still learn a lot about a product by reading the label. A lot of the labels have on specific words like caution, warning or danger that will indicate just how toxic the product is. Products that have poison or danger on the label tend to be the most toxic, the ones that are labeled with warning are fairly toxic and the ones with caution tend to be the least toxic. If you are able to however, try to find the products that do not have any of those signal words on the label.

In addition to those words there is usually an accompanying phrase that describes what harm the product can do. It may state that it causes burns on contact or that the vapors are harmful or even that it is flammable or may irritate the skin. Ensure that you read the instructions on how to use the product safely. There are a few labels that will list out the products active ingredients and this can really help you to determine what the irritating or caustic ingredients are.

If you are evaluating the ecological claims, look for certain things. For instance the phrase biodegradable does not have the same meaning as biodegradable in 5 days. Most substances will eventually break down over time under the right conditions. Natural or ecologically friendly also does not have the same meaning as plant based, no phosphates or no solvents. If the ingredients are on the label, look for the ones that do not contain petroleum based ingredients but plant based instead.

To cut back on dealing with excessive packaging try to find cleaners that you can buy in bulk. Try to find the ones that are placed in recycled containers. When you opt to do this you are supporting the companies that are recycling products. Also try to select cleaners that have no more than twenty percent of water in it. The undiluted cleaners do not require as much packaging and also attract less shipping costs.

What to Look For

Stay away from the cleaners that have poison or danger on the label. Also be wary of the ones that state that the product may cause burns or is corrosive.

The other products to be avoided would have ingredients like ammonia or chlorine listed as active ingredients as these can cause skin irritation and will also produce fumes that are toxic when they are combined.

You can also do more for the environment by refusing to purchase detergents that have phosphates in them as this will lead to the production of alkylphenol ethoxylates or algal blooms and this can threaten aquatic life and negatively affect the quality of water. The difficult thing about this is that these ingredients are not often listed on the labels. Certain brands though are APE and phosphate free. You just have to look for them.

Another thing to be wary of are unregulated claims. Unless the words eco friendly and natural come with further statements that indicate that no phosphates are included or that it is non toxic or solvent free then it really means nothing. Also note that some products that claim that they are organic may not be safer than a lot of the chemical based products out there.

Of course when you go to the supermarket, the term organic refers to foods that are not grown with pesticides. In chemistry it is the carbon based chemicals (volatile organic compounds included), that may cause cancer or brain damage as they release harmful fumes.

Karen S. Roberts

The main point here is that it is extremely important to do your research and find out exactly what is in the products that you are purchasing to use to clean your home or office. It is better to be safe than sorry in this case!

ABOUT THE AUTHOR

Karen S. Roberts has written on a myriad of topics but one of her favorite niches is the natural cleaning niche. She is not an astute environmentalist but she does believe in doing her part to protect the environment and prevent it from being destroyed any further. One of the things that she supports is the use of natural cleaning products as they not only protect the environment but they are also a much safer alternative for humans and animals alike.

These products can not only be used in the home but can be used in the offices as well. If something stronger is required then there are chemical based alternatives that are not extremely hazardous. Karen outlines all this and more in her book.

CPSIA information can be obtained at www.ICGtesting.com
Printed in the USA
LVOW05s0017070215

426097LV00007B/23/P